# RENTAL PROPERTY INVESTING MADE EASY

*From Poverty to Abundance*

By

## Christina Reynolds

# Contents

# Introduction

I nvesting in Real Estate has been one of the best decisions I have made. I purchased my first rental property in 2013 after my employer laid me off, so this forced me to figure out a way to create additional income. Although I ended up finding another job in the corporate world, I was devastated at the time; looking back now; I am thankful for the layoff because it pushed me into purpose. The experience I have gained throughout the years has allowed me to teach others what I have learned. Anyone can invest in real estate. You don't have to be a real estate agent, have any type of degree, or business license to invest in real estate.

The majority of the people I knew in my neighborhood growing up were renters. Living close to or beneath the poverty level was normal as I grew up; I did not realize it at the time because I grew up in a happy home. Now wiser, I understand that poverty is about the type of mindset a person has; if you think you will always be poor and struggle, then most likely, you will. Although I became pregnant at the age of 16, I didn't allow that to prevent me from pursuing my goals and dreams. Something inside of me has always yearned for more.

I was determined not to adapt to what I saw in my surroundings. The equity and appreciation of my first investment property have allowed me to get other properties. My tenant's rent makes the monthly mortgage payment and purchases other properties for me. Investing in real estate has allowed me to no longer struggle financially; it has allowed me to transition into a life of abundance. Everyone has a different definition of abundance; abundance to me means options. I still have my corporate job in which I love; however, real estate allows me to create passive income. I have learned that you can still work on things you are passionate about and work a full-time job. You have to first decide on whether you are interested in buying and holding (rental properties), flipping, or both. You may decide that you don't want to purchase rental properties because that will require you to have tenants, or you may decide that you don't want to flip properties because it doesn't allow you to create passive income. Sometimes people ask me which one they should do first, and it all depends on their goals and which one makes sense financially at the moment. Being an investor is a numbers game, and I look at each house I purchase as a business transaction; in the world of real estate, we do not get attached to houses. Making decisions regarding purchases are all about creativity and thinking outside the box. There are many ways to make money as an investor. Some other options include wholesaling properties, purchasing mobile homes with cash, and selling them to someone else with a rent to own option, tax liens, and taking over someone's mortgage payment and renting the house out to someone without taking out a mortgage in your name. My specialty is purchasing rental properties, but eventually, I want to venture out into flipping properties. After I made my first purchase, I knew that I wanted to invest long term; it became addictive.

# Chapter One

# Obtaining a Down Payment

Most people decide not to purchase a house or an investment property because they think you need a substantial amount of money to put down. Some people may also believe that the down payment funds have to come from one source. I purchased all my properties as a single mother, so I like to tell everyone that if I can do it, so can they. All it takes is planning and making sacrifices. There are several ways to come up with a down payment for an investment property and money for repairs. The funds can be obtained by using a personal line of credit, signature loan, cash advances on credit cards, 401K loans/withdrawals, and loans from family members. The down payment can include a combination of these options. Cash advances on a credit card are only recommended if the interest is 0.00%, and you have 12 months or more before interest rates start to accrue. Some investors get started by using OPM (other people's money). You can meet people at REIA (Real Estate Investment Association) meetings that are looking to invest their money with real estate investors; these people are known as private investors. Some people also take out home equity loans or home equity lines of credit on their primary residence to come up with the funds. I prefer getting signature loans and personal lines of credit through a credit union because their interest rates are usually lower for those types of loans.

Most mortgage companies require a down payment of 20% for a single-family property and 25% for a multi-family property for conventional loans. In addition to the down payment you will also be responsible for paying closing cost. Closing cost are expenses and fees you pay when you close on a house. The typical amount for closing cost is 2 to 5 percent of the loan amount. Closing cost applies to all loan types so discuss with your lender the maximum amount of closing cost they allow the seller to pay on your behalf. Always ask the seller to pay all or most of the closing cost. It is up to the seller to decide if they want to assist with the closing cost, but you never know until you try. Putting 20% down or more on a mortgage prevents PMI (Private Mortgage Insurance). A multi-family property includes a duplex, triplex, quadplex, and mixed-use properties. Mixed-use properties include a combination of residential and commercial space; they are usually near community amenities, which makes them desirable. The commercial space will allow you to generate a higher return on your investment because you can charge more for rent. If you purchase and live in a single-family house or multi-family property using an FHA loan, you will only be required to put 3.5% down. Still, you cannot have multiple FHA loans outstanding like you can with a conventional loan. There are a few exceptions to having multiple FHA loans outstanding at one time, so please reference Hud.gov for specific guidelines.

I increased my portfolio by purchasing houses as an owner occupant. Owner occupant means I lived in the homes for 12 months or greater, and then I moved out and rented the house to a tenant. This method required me to put 3.5%-10% down since I occupied the single-family home instead of purchasing them as investment propertieser. I had to make my homeowner's insurance company aware that I was no longer occupying the property so they could change the type of policy I had. I did not have to take any additional actions, such as obtaining a real estate or business license, when this transition had taken place. You can also purchase a property and live in it by using a conventional loan, which requires a down payment starting at 3% or a VA Loan, which requires 0% down. VA loans are offered to former or current military service members. You can live in the properties and then transition them into rental properties. Each lender has specific requirements, so you will need to verify the details with them.

## Chapter Summary/Key Takeaways

Obtaining the funds for repairs and the down payment for your investment property can come from many different sources. When you are comparing the options from the sources mentioned, keep in mind the cost (interest rates/fees), you will be charged because those amounts will be deducted from your total profit. Now that you have the funds for your down payment in the next chapter, you will learn how to locate a lender that can finance the investment property.

# Chapter Two

## Locating a Lender

Throughout my journey as an investor, I've had a great experience with the lenders I select. Some lenders weren't able to assist me because they were either asking for a high down payment or because they didn't finance properties in my price range. That didn't prevent me from reaching my goals, so I continued to persevere and search until I found the lender that would fit my needs. The interest rates, a term of the loan, down payment amount, and the amount you are required to have in reserves will vary depending on the lender or mortgage company. A lender is a company that finances the investment property for you. The lender serves the same purpose as a mortgage company. Reserves consist of a lender wanting you to have several months of mortgage payments on all your properties in an account. You can even have these funds in your 401K plan; they do not require you to use these funds; they just want to ensure you have these funds in some type of account. The lender I used required me to have three months' worth of reserves in an account.

Before making a purchase, I call around and gather that information, so when I am ready to make a purchase, I already know which company I am going to select. I also make sure I am getting a fixed interest rate because when you get an adjustable interest rate, most likely, your mortgage payment will increase throughout the loan. I also obtained a pre-approval letter so I could know how much I was approved for before I started searching for properties. Pre-approvals are usually good for 90-120 days. Most mortgage companies will only finance investment properties for a term of 15 years, and some lenders have a minimum amount they will finance, so it is important to inquire about that as well. When I called a few lenders, I realized that most of them want finance properties that are $50,000 or less. I was successfully able to locate a credit union that financed my first rental property for $47,500. Knowing an estimate of your credit score is valuable information to have when you are making calls to different lenders. Most lenders will approve you for a loan with a minimum credit score of 580. It is a great idea to aim for a higher credit score because as your score increases, your interest rate will decrease. Having a lower interest rate will allow you to save money. Usually, small local banks and credit unions are more lenient with the approval process.

You can also make attempts to call lenders in surrounding cities or different states. You can gather referrals for different lenders by joining and asking other investors on Real Estate Investment groups on Facebook and connecting with other investors via Facebook. Several people that have an interest in Real Estate have also reached out to me via LinkedIn, so that is a great way to connect. There is also a website called Meetup and it will allow you to locate Real Estate Networking groups in your area. Most cities have a Real Estate Investment Association (REIA), which will allow you to network with others that have an interest in real estate. Those meetings consist of real estate investors, lenders, contractors, real estate agents, and people that are looking to invest their money in real estate. Hard money lenders are popular in the world of investing in real estate. Hard money lenders are lenient and flexible when it comes to their approval requirements. Although their interest rates are higher, they will give you a loan with a lower credit score and higher debt-to-income when compared to traditional banks. Hard money lenders are extremely popular for investors that flip properties. The process of flipping a property includes purchasing, rehabbing, and selling the property for a profit.

## Chapter Summary/Key Takeaways

Locating the right lender for the deal is an important part of the process. Each lender has different terms and guidelines, so you have to figure out which lender is best to purchase from based on their interest rates and the term of the loan. Selecting a longer term will allow you to have a lower mortgage payment, and that is equivalent to a higher profit. Selecting a shorter term will allow you to pay the mortgage off quicker. Your selection should be based on your short-term and long-term goals. Once you have selected a lender and completed the approval process, then you can proceed with locating a property; this process will be discussed in the next chapter. I think looking for properties is the exciting part because it makes me feel like I am close to the finished line.

# Chapter Three

## Locating Properties

L ocating the perfect investment property takes time because you are competing against other investors and owner-occupants. I have always located all of my properties on my own; I used a real estate agent to handle the negotiations and to allow me to view the properties. I located the properties by viewing the websites that are located later in this chapter. I searched for my properties in the morning, on my lunch breaks, and when I got off of work. As soon as I identified a property that I was interested in, I called my real estate agent immediately to schedule an appointment for viewing because there are times when the houses sell quickly. There are several ways to locate rental properties. One of the traditional methods is to find a Real Estate Agent. The seller is responsible for paying the Real Estate Agent, so you do not have to worry about those costs. Locating the right agent is important because time is of the essence when trying to find a property. After all, you are competing against owner-occupants and other real estate investors. You can ask family and friends to give you referrals. Once you locate an agent, have a list of questions to ask. You want to verify the days and times they are available to show you properties. You want to find out their turn around time when it comes to responding to your text message, emails, and messages you leave on their voicemail. It's better to find an agent that is also an investor because they can identify great investment properties. Driving around for abandoned properties is another method. This method is also known as driving for dollars. Sometimes these properties can be identified because the windows are boarded up, the grass is long, and there is junk in the front yard. You can locate the owners of these properties by calling or going on the website for the city and county and looking up the property tax information. Once the owner has been identified, you can write them a letter asking them to purchase the property. These deals are also known as off-market deals if a Real Estate Agent is not involved. Most advanced investors use this method because they do not want to involve an agent so they can negotiate the deal and because the seller doesn't have to pay an agent to possibly get a better deal. Their experience in investing and the relationships they have with contractors gives them the ability to identify good deals. Deals can also be located by obtaining a list of properties for sale from wholesalers, probate court, and a probate attorney.

You can also locate off-market deals by visiting listsource.com and listability.com. I have not used those websites, but I have heard them mentioned by several other investors. In addition, go to websites hudhomestore.com and homepath.com; the houses on these websites include foreclosed homes that were owned by people that had government loans. I have always located my properties by visiting websites such as Redfin and Zillow. Once I discover a property, I call my agent and request a viewing. Once I find a property of my liking, I always get an inspection so I can have an idea of the repairs that are needed, and that also allows me to negotiate based on the findings in the inspection report. The reports are usually around $300-$400, but it could save you thousands in the long run if you purchase a property and are clueless to the major renovations that may be needed in the future.

Attend your local zoning meeting so you can find out about current and future projects. If they mention that they have plans to gentrify an area or a major corporation is coming to a particular area in the future, it will be a great idea to purchase a property or land in that area before the values increase. Once the development takes place, your investment will be worth a lot more. Finding a mentor is important because they can direct you in the right path and tell you about their mistakes. Although some mentors charge for their services, the valuable information gained from having a mentor can save you thousands of dollars, so they are well worth the investment. They can also give you access to their contractors, lending companies, real estate attorneys, tax accountants, and places that will allow you to purchase material at a discounted price. After your first investment property, you may want to consider purchasing a property in areas where investment properties are under $50,000. These locations include Cleveland, Ohio, Detroit, Michigan, Memphis, TN, Birmingham, Alabama, and Jacksonville, FL.

## Chapter Summary/Key Takeaways

As you can see, there are many options when it comes to locating the perfect property. When I came across properties that needed multiple repairs / renovations, I looked at them as if they were a diamond in the rough. You can always turn the properties into what you would like for them to be.

You must decide if you want to purchase a property that does or doesn't need repairs. You can purchase a property that is turnkey ready, which means that the investment property can be rented out immediately after the purchase; repairs or renovations are not required for these property types. The next chapter will give insight on properties that need repairs and they will allow you to have a higher return on your profit.

# Chapter Four

## Buy Low & Rent High

Several strategies can be used when purchasing rental properties. The first method I would like to discuss is buying a house for about $20,000- $30,000 with cash. I recommend locating a contractor to view the house with you and give an estimate on the costs for repairs prior to the making the purchase. I would also get an inspection after purchasing the home. You can spend about $15,000 or the minimum amount on repairs (material and labor) and put it on section 8 housing. Section 8 programs are managed by the Urban Development and the U.S. Department of Housing. The rental amounts that are paid out under the Section 8 program are usually higher than the market rental rates. Once the tenant is in place, you can get a home equity loan and use the cash to repeat the process. After you refinance the property, you will have a mortgage, and the estimated monthly payment on a home equity loan for $30,000 is $280 a month. The approximate amount you can get from section 8 depends on the area and number of bedrooms.

Let me give you an example of how your money can work for you instead of you working for the money. The average amount that Section 8 pays for a three-bedroom house in an area that I lived in is around $950. Your profit per house is about $670. Regardless of the loan type in the world of real estate, financing and renovations are a tedious/time-consuming process. Once your tenant moves in, the income you make turns into passive income. Passive incomes allow you to earn money while requiring you to do a minimum amount of work; it allows you to make money in your sleep. Most of what you will be doing is making required repairs and renovations. In some instances, the value of houses does not appreciate, but your ROI (Return on Investment) is higher. I plan on diversifying my portfolio and getting houses that fit this scenario in the future. My houses have a lower ROI, but their value appreciates so I can obtain a home equity loan and use those funds to purchase another property. When evaluating the profit on a property, you can use the 1% rule. The rule says that you should bring in 1% of the sales price for the monthly rental income. If a property costs $95,000, the monthly rental amount should be $950.

## Chapter Summary/Key Takeaways

As you can see, financing properties isn't the only option; purchasing properties with cash is another option. Placing a property under the Section 8 program is a way to guarantee that you will receive the portion of the rental income that is paid by the government each month. The Midwest, in general, is also a great place to look when trying to locate a property that has a low sales price. Purchasing a property with a low sales price or even buying a house with cash will allow you to profit more. In the next chapter, you will learn about equity and how it gives you the ability to purchase additional properties.

# Chapter Five

# Immediate Equity

You can also determine if you should purchase a house by looking at the sales history and forecast. This information will show you if the value of the property has increased over the years and if the value of the property will continue to increase in the future. If you complete the repairs instead of paying someone to do them, it is called sweat equity. Some investors purchase material in bulk so they can receive a discounted price. The materials purchased can be used in multiple properties. The materials can be kept in a storage building or a storage unit so you can focus more on purchasing rental properties and renovations and less time on selecting the material. You can also invite friends and family over to assist with some of the projects, and this will save you money. Giving them food and playing music makes it more enjoyable. You can live in this house for two years and then sell it. When you are working on a project, keep a record of everything, including the mileage and receipts, about the project, so you won't become overwhelmed when it is time to do your income taxes. For example, I place all of that information on an Excel Spreadsheet, and I tape my receipts to a white sheet of paper and made copies because receipts do fade. Once the copies are made, you can scan and email the documents to your email address. QuickBooks® is also a great tool to use to keep up with your expenses.

Living in a house for 24 months and then selling it can prevent you from paying capital gain taxes depending on your profit amount. You will need to talk to a tax professional or do some additional research on the maximum profit amounts you can make before being taxed. I know of people that have been successful in repeating this process a few times until they became finically free. I plan on incorporating this method in the future. Just think how quickly you can transition into a life of abundance if you can make $25,000-$35,000 every few years by using this method. If I sell any of my investment properties, I will have to pay a capital gains tax up to 30%. I do have the option to place the funds into a 1031 exchange account until it is time for my next project. The 1031 Exchange allows investors to defer paying taxes on a rental property when it is sold as long as the profits go toward a similar property. Another option is to refinance the investment property and get cash out or take out a home equity loan. The cash you receive can be used to put down on your next investment property.

## Chapter Summary/Key Takeaways

The equity in a property gives you the ability to continue to build your real estate portfolio. I have taken out a home equity loan on one of my properties; I used those funds to renovate one of my other properties. The funds from a home equity loan can also be used if an emergency comes up in your personal life, as a portion of your child's college tuition, or to renovate the house you live in at the time. The equity in a house can be beneficial for several reasons. I try to determine an estimate of the equity I can have in a house when I am searching for an investment property. The more equity I have in a property means the more money I can have access to if I need it; that also means I am maximizing my profit. In the next chapter, I will give you different ways on how to maximize your profit.

# Chapter Six

# Maximizing Your Profit

Investing in real estate allows you to be creative and to maximize your profits by using different strategies. The bigger the profit means the more money you make. Having a bigger profit allows you to save more money to put down on your next purchase, to save, or to invest in the stock market if you would like. For example, you can purchase three bedrooms with a basement and turn the basement into two additional bedrooms and place the house on Section 8. They are in high demand because there is shortage of 5 bedrooms, so providing a solution for large-size families and maximizing profits mean higher the profits because of more bedrooms. I have seen two-bedroom houses with additional space, and they could easily be transitioned into another bedroom by adding a wall, closet, and window. You must research the requirements in your state to determine what constitutes a bedroom. Being a real estate investor allows you to be creative, and this method will enable you to maximize your money. Just say, for instance, if the rental amount for a two-bedroom is $850, you will collect

$10,200 a year. If the rent amount is $1,150 for three-bedroom, you can collect $13,800. That is a difference of $3,600. If you want to take it a step further to see the magnitude of your profits, that $3,600 extra over five years is $18,000. When I purchase an investment property, I look at each purchase as a business transaction. I always analyze the deals to determine which one will bring me the highest return. Examples are listed below and on the next page. For the most part, you will only be required to occupy the property for 12 months, and then you can switch it to a rental property. The length of time to occupy a property may vary depending on the mortgage company and if you get down payment assistance. You will need to verify this with the mortgage company to determine the guidelines.

Single-Family Property - $95,000 Cost- Your lender requires you to pay a 20% down payment, so the mortgage payment, including closing cost, would approximately be $24,000. ($95,000 x 20%= $19,000 + $5,000/closing cost). The rental estimates for the properties in that area are expected to be $1,150 a month, and the estimated mortgage, including taxes, insurance, and repairs, is $800, so the property will produce a net income of $350 a month. The closing cost will vary depending on the lender.

Multi-Family Property (Conventional Loan-Not occupying the property)- $115,000 Cost- Your lender requires you to pay a 25% down payment so the mortgage payment including the closing cost would approximately be $34,750 ($115,000x25%= $28,750 + $6,000/closing cost). The rental estimates for the properties in that area are expected to be $800 month for each side ($1,600 total), and the estimated mortgage, including taxes, insurance, and repairs, is $900, so the property will produce a net income of $700 a month.

Multi-Family Property (FHA Loan- Occupying the property)- $115,000 Cost- Your lender requires you to pay a 3.5% as down payment including the closing cost would approximately be $10,025 ($115,000x3.5%= $4,025 + $6,000/closing cost). The rental estimates for the properties in that area are expected to be $800 month for each side ($1,600 total), and the estimated mortgage, including taxes, insurance, and repairs, is $900, so the property will produce a net income of $700 a month. Everything is the same as notated above; the only difference is the type of loan, down payment amount, and you will occupy one side of the property.

## Chapter Summary/Key Takeaways

Being a real estate investor gives you unlimited opportunities to be in control of your finances. You have some control over your profits and the amount you put down on the property just by the type of property and the loan type you select. Have you ever wondered what it would feel like to live in a house while someone else covered most or all your mortgage payments? This method is called house hacking, and additional details regarding the benefit of the method will be discussed in Chapter Seven.

# Chapter Seven

## House Hacking

Huse hacking is one of my favorite methods. Oh, how I wish I would have known about this method when I purchased my first investment property. House hacking allows you to save all or a portion of the money that you would normally pay for your rent or mortgage. You can use the saved funds to pay off a debt or put it towards your next investment property. The traditional definition of house hacking consists of purchasing a multi-family unit and living in one unit and renting the additional unit(s) out. The profits from the rent will cover most or all of the mortgage payments. Just continue to act as if you are still paying rent or a mortgage. For example, if you were previously paying $800 a month for rent or a mortgage when you weren't house hacking, then you can put that money in an account and act as if you are still liable for those amounts and in 3 years you will have $800x12= $9,600 / $9,600 x 3 years = $28,800 saved. That is the amount of money you can have saved by making a sacrifice to purchase your dream house first. House hacking has been taken to another level.

Some people have gone to the extreme of renting out available rooms in the house they are occupying. Just say if your current mortgage at your house is $900 a month and you have two bedrooms that are no longer being occupied, you can rent each of those bedrooms our for $450 each, and that will cover your mortgage.

You will have to decide if that will include utilities and cable. You are never too old or young to use this method, but I keep thinking if I started this method when I was much younger, I would be further along financially. I have talked to people regarding purchasing multi-family units, and they think that these properties are predominantly in inner-city areas, but that is not true. You can find these properties in non-inner-city areas. They come in the form of traditional duplexes; you can also purchase units that include one or two levels. There is also the option of buying a building that includes two townhomes; you will be the owner of both sides. If you are purchasing a multi-family unit, the tenant rental payments will count toward your income when a lender is trying to determine your approval amount.

# Chapter Summary/Key Takeaways

The house hacking method can be practiced anytime throughout your journey as an investor. The house hacking strategy method you select can also be changed at any moment. If you have kids in the house, you may not want to rent out rooms and select the multi-family option. House hacking gives you the ability to pay a minimum amount for the mortgage while having funds left over to save for your next property. Has the cost of repairs prevented you from making a purchase? If this has been your concern, there is a loan type that exists that will loan you up to $35,000 for repairs. This loan type will be discussed in the next chapter.

# Chapter Eight

# FHA (203 K Loan)

An FHA loan is a mortgage that is issued by the government (Federal Housing Administration). You have an option to obtain an FHA loan on a property, or you can get an FHA 203K loan; a down payment of 3.5% will be required for each loan type. The 203K loan allows homeowners to take out one loan for the purchase of a home and renovations on your primary residence. A total amount of up to $35,000 can be financed into the mortgage for the upgrades and repairs. Just because a lender offers an FHA loan does not mean they offer the FHA 203K loan, so you will need to locate a 203K lender if you decide on that option. Additional information regarding this loan type and lenders can be located at www.hud.gov. A 203K loan can also be used to purchase a HUD foreclosed home. You can visit www.hudhomestore.com for a list of HUD foreclosures, and it will tell you which properties are eligible for the 203K loan. A 203K loan is a great option because it prevents you from paying out of pocket for renovation costs. Once the renovations are complete, the value of the property will automatically increase, which means you have equity in the property. This loan option can also be used on single-family houses and one-to-four-unit properties. The 203K loan types usually require more paperwork when compared to your traditional FHA or Conventional loan, but the overall benefit will make it worth your while. You must occupy the house as your primary residence for 12 months before you sell or rent it out.

## Chapter Summary/Key Takeaways

I just found out about the 203(k) loan in 2019. I thought it was an amazing option because you don't have to pay out of pocket for renovations, and you don't have to locate contractors because the program will assign you a 203(k) Consultant that will assist you with the entire process. As previously mentioned, there are many options for investing in real estate. If you just aren't sure if rental property investing is something you want to do, you can experiment by renting a property for a shorter term or renting out rooms. This method will be discussed in the next chapter.

# Chapter Nine

## Shared Housing / Short Term Rentals

Shared housing and short-term rentals are great ways to maximize your money in the world of real estate. Renting out rooms to individuals allows you to make more money. This method can work anywhere, but it is popular in areas near colleges and big cities. The example below is an illustration of how you can make hundreds more each month by renting to an individual versus a family. The scenario used is for a three-bedroom two-bathroom house. The utilities for the tenants in the shared unit can be split between the tenants. You can also take the same scenario and rent to travel nurses and blue or white-collar workers that are looking for temporary housing. Several online market place platforms will allow you to list your property on their website. Some websites will allow you to locate a roommate or find a room that is for rent. These websites can be located by doing a Google search using the keywords short term rentals, vacation rentals, locating roommates. Those options will also allow you to vacation at the property and let your friends and family members use them if necessary. Shared housing can be considered another form of house hacking if you decide to live in one of the rooms. If you already pay for internet service, cable, or Netflix, you can give them access to those options for an additional cost.

Rental Amount-Single Family: $1,300 a month x 12 months a year = $15,600 Gross Income

Rental Amount-Shared Housing- $750 for the large room with bath, $650, for the next bedroom, and $550 for the small room- $1950 a month x 12 months a year = $23,400 Gross Income

## Chapter Summary/Key Takeaways

Short term rentals give you the ability to make a bigger profit. You can also use your short-term rental as a vacation house and allow your friends and family to use it. I am sure the 2020 Coronavirus (COVID-19) pandemic had a negative financial impact on owners of short-term rentals because a lot of people were staying home. Coming up with some type of alternative plan in case something like this happens again is always a good idea. If I had a short-term rental, I would probably convert it into a long-term rental so I could continue to receive enough income to cover the mortgage. This is one of the creative components of being a real estate investor.

Selecting a good tenant can make your investment journey smooth or challenging. I couldn't ask for better tenants; they take care of my property, and they pay the rent on time. The next chapter will provide you with information on the tenant screening process.

# Chapter Ten

## Screening Tenants

Selecting a tenant to occupy your property is very important. The wrong tenant can cost you thousands of dollars in repairs and court costs. Investing in real estate and selecting tenants is a risk, but you never know what type of experience you will have until you try. I have been fortunate to have chosen the right tenants throughout my journey. A few major repairs were needed at some of my rental properties throughout the years. These repairs included replacing the HVAC system and ductwork under the house due to a rodent infestation. I have always encouraged my tenants to call me when a repair is needed. If I visit a property and notice that a repair is needed I take immediate action to ensure that it is fixed. It is important to take care of your rental properties because it prevents the value from decreasing due to neglect. When I rented my first property as a tenant, it made me feel good to rent from a landlord that took care of the property; it made me want to take care of the property even more. I have also decided to provide my tenants with the same excellent service. It is a great idea to have a credit card available and cash saved for those unexpected repairs.

In screening for potential tenants, you can call the courthouse to verify if they had previous evictions. Some counties have websites that allow you to verify if a person has lawsuits in civil court from previous landlords and creditors. I was informed by another landlord that when he screens tenants, he asks them if he can view the property they are currently renting just to verify if they are taking care of the property. Background and credit checks can be done by using an online tenant screening company. The fees for these services will be paid by the applicant when they pay the application fee. Entering the applicant's name along with the cities/states they lived in on the internet may also provide valuable information. Once a tenant has moved in, you can conduct monthly or quarterly inspections. You can create a checklist and provide the tenant with a copy. You can check the air filters, appliances, and fire alarms to ensure they are working correctly. You can also volunteer to provide the tenant with free air filters for the first three months, and so when you go by to change them, you can tell early on if they are taking care of the property.

Having tenants qualify to move into your property makes your selection fair and nonbiased. If a tenant is late, you can charge a late payment; the percentage for each state is different. It is my understanding that if a tenant is a participant of the section 8 program them, you can only charge them a late fee for the portion of the rent they are paying. When I select a tenant, I do not solely base my decision on their credit score, work history, income, previous rental history, or criminal background. I consider everything. If someone has a low score due to medical bills, but they have paid everything else on time, I would still consider them. Also, if someone has something on their criminal background, but it was ten years ago, I would consider them. Providing my tenants with a house in great condition and a safe community puts a smile on my face. Being a landlord allows me to be a decision-maker; it also allows me to be a blessing. It allows me to waive late fees and waive the prorated rent amount if they do not move in during the beginning of the month. Most landlords want to consider these perks, but that is one of the things that separate me from other landlords.

## Chapter Summary/Key Takeaways

Selecting great tenants has allowed my journey as an investor to be stress-free; they continue to allow me to generate passive income. My tenants only call me if there is a need for a repair, and that is not often. Screening a tenant is an important part of the process because selecting a tenant that isn't good can cost you unnecessary time and money. After your tenant has moved in, you should be able to relax and enjoy the profits.

# Conclusion

Now that you have an idea of how to get started, you have a decision to make. Hopefully, you decide to take a leap of faith in making your first purchase. I truly understand that everything is not for everyone, if you decide that investing is not for you there are programs that will help you with most or all of the down payment and closing cost if you want to occupy the property and not rent it out. If you need assistance in funding as an investor use your community resources. Some cities offer Community Development Block Grants for investors; they assist with funding the renovations for investment properties.

As an investor, I receive rental income, provide coaching, and soon will teach classes and lunch and learns all from my passion. When you do something that you enjoy and get paid, it doesn't feel like work. If you are currently employed, you can save a portion of that income and put it toward your dream fund. If you decide to proceed with investing in real estate, it is a great idea after you purchase your first few properties to start researching getting an LLC, business account, and business credit. You can also begin to determine what type of properties you want to purchase and find your niche.

The steps toward purchasing a rental property include making sure you have the down payment funds, having the appropriate credit score, and research. Always have a contingency plan in place just in case things doesn't work out as planned. The Coronavirus (COVID-19) pandemic of 2020 is a prime example; unfortunately, this has caused a lot of people to lose their jobs, and they weren't able to pay their rent at all or on time. That is one reason why it is essential to have an emergency fund, a personal line of credit, or a credit card that allows you to have access to cash advances.

I have learned that wealthy people create a business or invest their money in real estate and allow their profits to purchase their liabilities. For example, profits from one property can pay for a car note, and profits from another property can pay the mortgage on a primary residence. If I can purchase multiple properties of the income of a single mom while working a full-time job, anyone can do it. As you can see, real estate investing isn't complicated. It takes dedication, discipline, and resilience to live an abundant lifestyle by investing in real estate.

# Glossary

**Assessed Value:** This value is determined by a county tax assessor, and the purpose is to calculate your property taxes.

**Portfolio Loan:** A mortgage that investors use when they are financing several properties under a single loan.

**Interest Rate:** A monthly mortgage is typically composed of interest and principal payments on a loan. The cost your mortgage company charges for borrowing your money is called an interest rate. A fixed interest rate does not change, and an adjustable-rate goes up and down. A mortgage payment usually consists of the interest and principal. I only select fixed interest rates because I do not want my mortgage payment fluctuating to a high amount due to a high adjustable rate.

**Appraised Value:** This value is determined by a licensed appraiser, and it consists of gathered data and the judgment of the appraiser. This value is used by the bank for lending.

**Market Value:** This value can be determined by anyone. This value can be determined by active property listings and the history of sold properties.

**Cash Reserves:** Reserves include the balance that you have saved after you close on your house. This type of balance can be considered an emergency fund. If you lose your job, you will still be able to afford your mortgage payments.

Escrow: An escrow account includes your property taxes and homeowner's insurance. These funds are combined with your mortgage payment.

**Buyer's Agent:** A buyer's real estate agent represents the buyer in the homebuying process, and a listing real estate agent represents the seller.

**Private Mortgage Insurance:** This type of insurance is usually required when a buyer puts less than twenty percent down on a home. The PMI can be satisfied with a Conventional Loan once the homeowner reaches twenty percent equity. USDA and FHA loans require a different type of mortgage insurance. VA loans do not require mortgage insurance. You can request in writing that the PMI is removed once your balance drops to 80% of your home's value.

# Acknowledgments

I would like to first thank my Lord and Savior Jesus Christ for placing it on my heart to write this book and giving me the passion for investing in real estate. I give thanks to my mother, Patricia Hill, who has always believed in me and told me to dream big even. She told me big things were coming my way even when I didn't believe it or see it. Early on, my family and friends have supported me throughout the years. They supported all of my business ventures and listened to all of my goals and dreams. For that, I thank them. To my sisters Kenwana and Kenkaysha, you never doubted me once and supported me from the beginning, and I am thankful for that. To my brother Rodney, thanks for being supportive. I would like to give a special thanks to Dr. Lanise Hutchins, my friend, my editor, and one of my role models. When I first mentioned writing this book, you didn't hesitate to offer your assistance despite your busy schedule, and I greatly appreciate it. To my amazing daughters, Ashya, and Richelle, you have been my biggest cheerleaders. You have inspired me in so many ways and encouraged me to step out of my comfort zone, and I love you'll dearly. To everyone that has everyone that believed and supported me at any point and time no matter how big or small I give thanks.

# About the Author

Christina Reynolds currently resides in Atlanta, GA, and has a Bachelor's Degree in Business Administration. She has a passion for helping people reach their dreams by giving them the resources to purchase their first house and investment property. She likes teaching people the basics of financial literacy while providing tips and suggestions to people so they can improve their credit score. Christina enjoys spending time with her daughters (Ashya and Richelle), family, and friends.

Follow Christina on Instagram at
https://www.instagram.com/tinathehomeinvestor/

# Disclaimer

This book was created for informational purposes only, and I am not an attorney or a CPA (certified public accountant). Any suggestions, ideas, or examples given are solely my opinion based on my experience and research. You should seek the advice of an attorney and CPA before investing in real estate. Anyone that reads this book is advised to do their due diligence when purchasing an investment property. Reading this disclaimer confirms that you agree that the company and I are not responsible for the outcome of the decision you make about investing in real estate.

www.ingramcontent.com/pod-product-compliance
Lightning Source LLC
Chambersburg PA
CBHW070920210326
41521CB00010B/2251